21

DAY

FAST

21 DAYS THAT WILL REVOLUTIONIZE YOUR LIFE!

BOB RODGERS

ISBN: 0-939241-93-5

THE 21-DAY FAST

Published by:
Bob Rodgers Ministries
P. O. Box 19229
Louisville, KY 40259

THE 21-DAY FAST

Table of Contents

The 21-Day Fast

FOREWORD

The purpose of *"The 21-Day Fast"* is to share the power that will explode in your life as you add fasting to your prayers. Another purpose is to help you prepare and give guidelines for your fast of 21 days.

There is never a good time to fast. In the winter, it is too cold. In the summer, it is too hot. There is always a special dinner or birthday to keep us from fasting. I suggest that you just fast and everything will work out.

A great time to start a 21 day fast is at the beginning of the year. First of all, you set the course of the year. When I pray in the morning, I set the course of my day. Nothing is going to happen to me outside of God's will when I pray at the beginning of the day.

Secondly, blessings will happen for you and your family throughout the year because you fasted in January. God will bless you in May, August, or in October. You will still receive blessings because you fasted at the beginning of the year.

Thirdly, you release the Matthew 6:33 principle, "Seek ye first the kingdom of God and His righteousness; and all these things will be added unto you." You are seeking God at the first of your year. Now get ready for "things" to "be added unto you."

When you participate in a 21-day fast, there are

thousands and thousands of believers all over the world who are fasting at the same time. When you begin to fast and "link" with them spiritually, the same blessings that are upon them and the same answers to prayer and spiritual breakthroughs that they receive, you receive also.

If one fasting person has a breakthrough, in their finances for instance, you will receive a financial breakthrough, too. When there is a breakthrough in the direction of their life, you will get a breakthrough in your life.

Your prayers are multiplied. Your prayer fasting is multiplied ... *"One can chase a thousand, two can put ten thousand to flight."*

One man's fast is very powerful. But two men's fast means multiplied strength and releases multiplied angels of God.

Be encouraged and inspired to follow God through your 21-day fast!

--Bob Rodgers

The 21-Day Fast

INTRODUCTION

WHY 21 DAYS?

You can experience 21 days of MIRACLES through prayer and fasting. The greatest miracles that I have ever experienced have come during periods of prayer and fasting.

What do you need from God?

My prayer is that during your days of prayer and fasting, you will experience the greatest breakthroughs of your life.

Jesus expects every person to fast. In Mark 2:20 He said, "Then shall they fast in those days." Matthew 6 declares, "When you give," "When you pray," and "When you fast." It doesn't say, "If you give," "If you pray," or "If you fast." Just as God expects you to give and to pray, He also expects you to fast.

You have a time to give, and that is when you go to church. Every Sunday you "bring your tithes and offerings into the store house." There are times you pray every day.

What about fasting? When do you fast?

The best time to fast for an extended time is at the beginning of the year. In fasting, you set the course of your entire year. Things happen to you in June or August that are often a result of fasting in January.

You are blessed the entire year because you sought God's direction and blessings in the beginning. It is the principle of Matthew 6:33.

I began fasting in the spring of 1973. I was pastoring a small church with a lot of problems. I had visited Korea and had seen 1,500 young people fasting for seven days at Prayer Mountain. This greatly inspired me. I could not fast even one day. In the afternoon I would get so hungry, I'd break my fast. Then I learned to fast half a day, which is until 3 p.m. Finally, I was able to fast for 24 hours, then three days, seven days, 21 days and now 40-days.

Every time I have fasted God has shown me something. Sometimes it has been a direct answer to prayer. At other times the Bible has become so alive and God has given me a *"rhema"* word. Then I have had visitations, visions and dreams. I want to share with you six life-changing lessons I have learned through fasting.

1. FASTING BREAKS POVERTY

Fasting breaks the power of poverty. To some this may come as a shock. But it is really true. I discovered that as I plant a seed each time I fast, a major blessing returns to me quickly. As I was reading the Bible that secret opened up to me.

Peter preached from the Book of Joel on the Day of Pentecost. The book begins by telling about a nation that was coming against Israel. They are *"strong, and without number; his teeth are the teeth of a lion." (Joel 1:6).*

He says it is the army of locust and palmer worms without number. They devoured the land, so there was no food to eat. Poverty had ravaged the entire country. Joel 1:13 says they were so poor they couldn't even bring an offering to the house of the Lord. Has this ever happened to you?

They called for a fast.

"Blow the trumpet in Zion, sanctify a fast, call a solemn assembly."

--Joel 2:15

As a result of the fast, "the threshing floors shall be full of wheat, and the vats shall overflow with new wine and oil." The "wheat" and "new wine" mean prosperity. God broke their poverty.

Joel 2:26 tells, *"You shall eat in plenty and be satisfied, and praise the name of the Lord thy God who has dealt wondrously with you."* The Lord brought great financial blessings as the people fasted and prayed.

Over the years I have seen many hundreds of people with low-paying jobs, people who couldn't afford a home or good automobile, and businesses facing financial troubles. God turned it around as they fasted and prayed. During the spring and summer, scores of couples in our church will be moving into new homes. It happens every year. The reason is because they have fasted in January. Get ready for a 30, 60 and a 100-fold blessing this coming year. Healings follow fasting.

2. FASTING BRINGS HEALING

Isaiah 58 is the chapter in the Bible that tells about

fasting, just as I Corinthians 13 talks about love. In this chapter it gives twenty of the greatest promises in the scriptures that happen when one fasts. Isaiah 58:8 says, *"Thine health shall spring forth speedily."*

During the first year our church began fasting corporately, we also began holding miracle services at the end of the fast. In our first miracle meeting a man came who was dying with cancer. He was a big man that had weighed more than 250 pounds. When he came for prayer, he was very frail and had not eaten for more than two weeks.

After we prayed for him, he returned to his seat. Five minutes later he said to his wife, *"Let's leave now." "Why, the service isn't over?" she said. "I am so hungry I must eat something now."* He went home and ate and slept. When he woke up, he ate again. God healed this man from cancer. That year, 37 people were healed of cancer. Expect healing miracles!

3. SEXUAL ADDICTIONS ARE BROKEN

Judges 19 and 20 tell of a young man form Judah whose wife was raped and murdered by a group of homosexuals. This sexual sin had gained control over many of the tribe of Benjamin. They were fighting to protect the Sodomites. God spoke to the armies to go up, but the Benjamites killed 22,000 men. They prayed again and went into battle. This time, 18,000 were killed. The third time they fasted and prayed. Then God gave them a glorious victory.

Sexual sins are some of the most difficult sins to get the victory over. Deuteronomy explains the sins of the father follow the son four generations. However, sexual sins can carry a curse for ten generations.

Fasting helps break the power of sexual addictions like pornography, homosexuality, masturbation, fornication, adultery and lust. A man came to me who was bound in homosexuality. He was married with children, but had lived this secret lifestyle since a 12-year-old boy.

I told him to fast for 21 days. He fasted with the church in January. God totally delivered him. He became a leader in our church and later was transferred out of town with his job. I never told anyone of his former lifestyle. It was amazing to see how God rescued his life.

4. GENERATIONAL CURSES BROKEN

"You shall raise up the foundations off many generations," states Isaiah 58:12. In other words, curses in your family—poverty, divorce, sickness and trouble—no longer follow to your children. The demonic attachment to your family can be broken. You can now raise up a family under the blessing and not under the curse.

While his children were young, Harold began fasting one day a week for his family. When his son asked him, "Dad, why don't you eat supper with us?" He replied, "I'm believing God for my family that divorce will never come to any member of our home. Also, God promised me all our children will be used in the ministry."

There were two sons and one daughter. The daughter married a very successful pastor and one son also trained for the ministry. The second son decided he wanted to be an engineer.

After two years at the university he called home one evening, *"Dad, I don't want to go into engineering. I believe God has called me to preach."*

God raised up a family of servants of God as the father fasted consistently for his home.

5. DEMON POWERS ARE BROKEN

Jesus said, *"This kind can come forth by nothing, but by prayer and fasting." (Mark 9:29). "This kind"* means there are *"other kinds."* Some demon powers are only cast out as people will fast.

I customarily fast one day each week.

On one of my fast days, a lady came to see me, telling me she was an intercessor in prayer. Instantly I sensed something was not right in my spirit. As I talked with her, it came out she was hearing voices that said it was the spirit of an intercessor. This was an evil spirit which had deceived this lady. The spirit was cast out and she was totally delivered.

You develop a sensitivity to spiritual things when you fast. Casting out devils is not necessarily a difficult thing, if you maintain a lifestyle of prayer and fasting.

6. GOD REVEALS THINGS TO COME

As you read of fasting in the Bible, it is often in a context of God giving a revelation to people. It was true when Daniel fasted 21 days, the angel Gabriel came and told him of things to come, including the very year Jesus was to be born. (Daniel 10).

It happened in Acts 13:14 when Paul and Barnabas *"ministered to the Lord, and fasted, the Holy Ghost said, Separate me Barnabas and Saul for the work whereunto I have called them."* They received the call to be apostles and plant churches when they fasted.

In Acts 10, Cornelius fasted. God told him to send for Peter and he would tell him what to do. At the same time that Peter was waiting to eat, God gave him a vision to go to the gentiles and preach the gospel.

Revelation comes when people fast. As I have sought God for this coming year, the scripture keeps coming to me in Acts 1:8, *"Ye shall receive power after that the Holy Ghost is come upon you and ye shall be witnesses."* I sense a new anointing is coming on the church for great miracles and soul-winning this coming year.

As you fast and pray, target unsaved family members, brothers and sisters, people you work with, neighbors and classmates. Put them on your prayer list and pull the blinders off their minds in prayer so they can see the truth of the gospel (2 Corinthians 4:4).

During these 21 days of prayer and fasting, it will not be a hard time, but a victorious time that will affect your future the entire year.

"I ate no pleasant bread, neither came flesh nor wine in my mouth, neither did I anoint myself at all, till three whole weeks were fulfilled."
--Daniel 10:3

Many people ask me, *"Why 21 days?"*

LENGTHS OF FASTS

During the past 30 years, I have discovered some dynamics concerning the length of a fast. There are breakthrough periods as you fast.

These breakthrough periods are:

1. A half-fast, or until 3:00 p.m.

2. A 24-hour fast

3. A three-day fast

I have fasted one day and fasted two days without seeing any difference. However, at the end of three days, a breakthrough takes place.

The next breakthrough is day seven. The next breakthrough is at 14 days, then 21 days, 30 days, and finally 40 days.

This may seem unusual and strange that there is length of days associated with spiritual victories in your life. However, this is the same dynamic that touches the tithe. God doesn't say give 6% or 8%. He says to give 10%.

He honors the tithe, the tenth. The miracle happens not at 8%, but when you give the entire tithe.

In the same way, there is Godly power released when you fast 21 days.

The number three has to do with the trinity—the

Father, Son, and Holy Ghost. This expresses holiness. The Covenant was between Abraham, Isaac, and Jacob. There is faith, hope, and charity. Proverbs declares that, *"A three-fold cord is not easily broken..."*. The number three is used a lot of times in the Bible.

Seven is the number of perfection. There are *seven* days in a week. Israel marched around Jericho *seven* times.

Multiply three times seven and you get 21—*"holy perfection."*

HOW I STARTED FASTING

The first time our church fasted 21 days I had just become the new pastor.

My father had died suddenly and the church was hopelessly and helplessly in debt. I really didn't know what to do. I asked the church to fast with me for 21 days.

The idea was to fast a meal a day for 21 days and to seek God's wisdom.

I had always fasted between Christmas and the New Year for one week. So I fasted for one week. That is three meals a day for seven days---21 meals.

However, after week one, the Lord impressed me to fast the second week. Then came the third week. I didn't think I could fast for 21 days, but God helped *me*.

Immediately, we began to see breakthroughs in the church.

There was a man who was laid off because his company was downsizing their work force. He was in his fifties. He had no work at all. He heard us talking about fasting over the radio. He came to the church on the first Sunday that we started on our 21-day fast. He had never fasted before, but he decided he was going to fast with us. He hadn't been able to get a job, as hard as he tried. That first week he fasted, he went out and found a job paying him more money starting out than where he had worked for years at this other company. God turned his situation around as he fasted and prayed.

Our finances doubled. The church began to multiply in attendance. That year, 37 people were healed from cancer!

Since that time the money of the church has almost tripled.

There is a man in our church that was fasting 21 days. On the 18th day of the fast, the Lord spoke to him and said, *"I am going to bless you!"* God asked him how much money he had. He responded, *"I've got $2,000!"*

The Lord said, *"Why don't you see what I can do with that $2,000!"* The next service he gave the $2,000 in the offering. About two days later, he was looking in the newspaper and saw an ad for some real estate/apartments. He made an offer on 25 units with owner financing. The seller was a doctor who had suffered a heart attack. He no longer wanted the pressure of the apartments. So he agreed to sell it to him.

The fellow borrowed $25,000 off credit cards for the down payment. In three months, there was a fire in a couple of the units. After the insurance settled with him, he was able to get the apartments fixed, and had $25,000 left over, and paid off the credit cards. God had given him those apartments free. He had been fasting 21 days.

God has added thousands of new people to the church. As you fast 21 days, expect holy perfection to take place in your life.

The 21-Day Fast

PREFACE

10 THINGS YOU SHOULD KNOW BEFORE YOU FAST!

"But thou, when thou fastest, anoint thine head, and wash thy face;"
--Matthew 6:17

1. **Headaches, bad breath, and run down feelings are signs that the fast is working.**

   During a time of fasting the body purifies itself and feeds off of impurities and pollutants in your body. After approximately three days, the headaches will begin to cease. After approximately five days, hunger will also stop.

2. **Fasting will not impair your health.**

   Throughout history fasting has been a prescribed method for healing. Animals cease to eat when they become ill.

   Hippocrates was an outstanding physician in his time. He is the *"father of modern medicine."* He set standards followed by doctors today called the "Hippocratic Oath". Hippocrates taught his students to rely on diet and exercise instead of drugs. He fasted often. He advised people to eat one meal a day.

3. Fasting increases a person's faith.

Romans 10:8 says, *"But what saith it? The word is nigh thee, even in thy mouth, and in thy heart: that is, the word of faith, which we preach."*

You talk and eat with the mouth. The mouth speaks faith and eats food. Some unbelief cannot be broken without fasting. Each day you fast your faith is increased; and your miracle will happen!

I had a friend who was Korean. He was the head of a Korean gang in New York City. He was arrested and sentenced to 25 years in prison. While he was in prison, a man came and preached. He began to visit him and led him to Christ. He said, *"Now the way to get great breakthroughs is through a fasting prayer."*

In about two weeks, the preacher came back to visit the Korean man in prison. His name was Park. Park said to him, *"You know I have been doing what you told me. I have been praying as fast as I can, but I do not see any results."* The fellow said, *"No, a fasting prayer is not about praying fast. It's about not eating. And Jesus fasted for 40 days."*

He asked him, *"What is the thing you would like to see God do for you more than any other thing?"* He said, *"Well, I would like to get out of prison, but I am sentenced for 25 years."* He said, *"Why don't you fast about it?"*

Park began to fast for 40 days. He had never fasted before. By the time he had fasted the first week, all he could think about was food. But after about a week, God really began to deal with him. God began to put his finger on certain things in his life, telling him, *"You've got to change this."* He greatly humbled himself to God. After 21 days, he was so weak that the prison officials took him and made him eat. So he ended his fast at 21 days.

Two weeks later, they released him from prison. He went back to New York and began to work with David Wilkerson for awhile. Then he began to minister to these gangs. One time, they even shot him because he was trying to break up a gang fight. He also went to Bible School. God brought a beautiful, wonderful Christian lady into his life. Today, he is in full-time ministry.

4. Drink plenty of fluids.

Bottled water should be taken in large quantities before and during the fast. This will help flush poisons and impurities out of your system. Approximately one gallon a day should be used in the cleansing process.

A man in Colorado read a book I had written on fasting. He started a 21-day fast and became deathly sick after 12 days. He telephoned me, saying, *"I don't know if I can finish the fast. I am so sick."*

"Are you drinking plenty of water?"

"Yes, right from the faucet."

"There is where the problem is. You are being poisoned by the chlorine." He started drinking bottled water and was fine.

5. Fasting is constant intercession before God.

When you fast you may not feel like praying. Intercessory prayer is not only a spiritual process, but a physical process. During a fast you may become weak and not feel like praying. But the fasting process is a constant prayer unto God.

6. Fasting strengthens your inner will.

Fasting increases your will power. Actually fasting is much more mental than physical. It makes a person tougher and stronger on the inside. Set your faith and don't waiver in what you are asking of God.

> *"But let him ask in faith, nothing wavering. For he that wavereth is like a wave of the sea driven with the wind and tossed.*
>
> *"For let not that man think that he shall receive anything of the Lord.*
>
> *"A double minded man is unstable in all his ways."*
>
> *--James 1:6-8*

7. Focus on the Word of God.

When Jesus fasted he was tempted by the devil. In every case he used the Word of God to overcome. Without exception, God has spoken to me through the scriptures each time I have fasted. When you become hungry, if you will read from the Word of God, it will satisfy your physical hunger.

8. Your prayers need to be specific.

I encourage you to write down your greatest needs. Pray specifically over each need during this time of fasting. As God impresses you with direction and guidance, jot down what God speaks. Keep a prayer journal to record your prayers and God's answers.

9. The victory often comes after the fast is over.

When Jesus was fasting he was tempted by the devil. The power of the Holy Spirit came upon Christ after the fast.

"And Jesus returned in the power of the Spirit into Galilee: and there went out a fame of him through all the region round about."   *--Luke 4:14*

There was a man in our church, Bill Miller, who was an airplane mechanic. He worked on the large 747's. He felt he should go on a 21-day fast. A year prior to going on this fast, he had lost some bridge work (teeth). He had searched all over his house. He finally went back to the dentist who made him some more bridge work.

After coming off the fast, he started coughing. He actually coughed up his dentures. He had swallowed them. They had been lodged in his lung for one year! Can you image the necessary surgery that would have probably developed and trouble that would eventually have happened if he had not fasted?

10. Wisdom should be used in breaking the fast.

There have been reported cases where people have

fasted for long periods of time and have broken their fast with meat and other foods that are hard to digest. This lack of wisdom has cost some people their lives. This is serious. Do not break your fast by eating meat and other hard-to-digest foods. Eat foods that are easy to digest.

The sooner the first meal passes through the body the more effect it has as it carries out poisons collected in the intestines and stomach. The best laxative foods are fresh, sweet fruits, such as grapes, cherries or raw vegetables.

Set aside this time of fasting in dedication to the Lord. Our purpose is to draw close to Him and receive His guidance. He will help you as you commit each day unto Him and pray.

The 21-Day Fast

PROLOGUE

PRE-FASTING DIET

"And the ravens brought him bread and flesh in the morning, and bread and flesh in the evening; and he drank of the brook."
--I Kings 17:6

Fasting brings you closer to God. It is also a way to humble yourself. There are also physical benefits, such as weight loss. Fasting must not to be confused with dieting.

Here is a pre-fasting diet that will help prepare your body for a long fast. It not only cleanses the body from poisonous toxins, but stimulates the metabolism of your body. Some have lost as much as 17 pounds in one week depending on one's body weight.

BASIC FAT BURNING SOUP:

6 large green onions (scallions)
2 green peppers   1 or 2 large cans of tomatoes
1 bunch of celery   1 large head of cabbage
1 package of Lipton Onion Soup mix

Season with salt, pepper, curry, parsley, etc., if desired, or six bouillon cubes. Half of this recipe was used by two people for four days. We kept it continually hot in a crock pot.

Cut vegetables in small to medium pieces and cover with water. Boil for ten minutes. Reduce to simmer and continue cooking until vegetables are tender.

This can be eaten anytime you are hungry. Eat as much as you want, whenever you want at any time of the day. This soup will not add calories. The more you eat, the more you lose. If eaten alone for indefinite periods, you would suffer malnutrition. Fill a thermos in the morning if you will be away during the day.

DAY ONE: All fruits except bananas. Your first day will consist of all the fruit you want, except bananas. Cantaloupes and watermelons are lower in calories than most fruits. Eat only your soup and fruits the first day. Drink unsweetened tea, cranberry juice or water.

DAY TWO: All vegetables. Eat until you are full with all the fresh, raw or cooked vegetables of your choice. Try to eat green, leafy vegetables and stay away from dry beans, peas and corn.

Eat all the vegetables you want along with your soup. At dinner time on this day reward yourself with a big baked potato and butter. Eat all the soup you want, but don't eat your fruits.

DAY THREE: Mix day one and day two. Eat all the soup, fruit, and vegetables you want. You cannot have a baked potato this day. On day three you should begin to lose weight. Eat as much soup as you can.

DAY FOUR: Bananas and skimmed milk. Eat as many as eight bananas and drink as many glasses of skimmed milk as you can on this day along with your soup. Bananas are high in calories; so is the milk. But, on this particular day your body will need the potassium and the carbohydrates, proteins and calcium to lessen your craving for sweets.

DAY FIVE: Beef and tomatoes (or salad). You may have 10-20 ounces. Try to drink as many as 6-8 glasses of water this day to wash away the uric acid in your body. Eat as much of the soup as you can.

DAY SIX: Beef and veggies. Eat beef and vegetables to your heart's content. You can even have two or three steaks if you like with green, leafy vegetables BUT NO BAKED POTATOES. Be sure to eat plenty of soup.

DAY SEVEN: Brown rice, unsweetened fruit juices and vegetables. Again, stuff, stuff, stuff yourself. Be sure to eat plenty of soup. If you have not cheated on your diet, you will find that you have lost 10-17 pounds. If you have lost more than 15 pounds, stay off the diet for two days before resuming.

This seven-day eating plan can be used as often as you like. As a matter of fact, if correctly followed, it will clean your system of impurities and give you a feeling of well-being as never before. After only a few days of this process, you will begin to feel lighter by at least 10 and possibly 17 pounds. You'll have an abundance of energy. Continue this plan as long as you wish and feel the difference.

This diet is a fast, fat-burning diet. You will burn more calories than you take in. It will flush your system of impurities and give you a feeling of well-being.

After day three, you will have more energy than

when you began, if you do not cheat. After being on the diet for several days, you will find your bowel movement has changed—eat a cup of bran and fiber. Although you can have black coffee with this diet, you may find you do not need the caffeine after the third day.

Definite "no-no's": No bread. No alcoholic beverages. No carbonated beverages. Drink water, unsweetened tea, black coffee, unsweetened fruit juices, cranberry juice.

Any prescribed medication will not hurt you on this diet. Continue this plan as long as you wish and feel the difference in both mental and physical disposition. If you prefer, you can substitute broiled fish for the beef on only one of the beef days. You need the high protein from the beef on at least one day.

(This diet is from Sacred Heart Memorial Hospital, New Jersey. It is used for overweight heart patients who need to lose weight rapidly, usually before surgery).

The 21-Day Fast

Chapter 1

DAY 1

THE PURPOSE OF FASTING

"And Cornelius said, Four days ago I was fasting until this hour; and at the ninth hour I prayed in my house, and, behold, a man stood before me in bright clothing."

--Acts 10:30

POWER. The Power of God is working in your life! *Matthew 1 – 5*

"According as his divine power hath given unto us all things that pertain unto life and godliness, through the knowledge of him that hath called us to glory and virtue:" *--2 Peter 1:3*

Fasting is a Biblical commandment that gets results. I have fasted for many years, and I have witnessed great miracles.

God expects you to fast to accomplish His purpose in YOUR life!

You may wonder why God would choose fasting to accomplish His purposes. Obviously, it is a wonderful way to get the flesh under control. But the purposes are many more than that one obvious reason. Take time to look up the scripture references and fully understand each purpose.

1. TO HUMBLE OURSELVES (OVERCOME THE FLESH).

"But as for me, when they were sick, my clothing was sackcloth: I humbled my soul with fasting; and my prayer returned into mine own bosom."   *--Psalm 35:13*

"When I wept, and chastened my soul with fasting, that was to my reproach."--Psalm 69:10

2. TO REPENT AND SEEK THE LORD.

"And it came to pass, while the ark abode in Kirjathjearim, that the time was long; for it was twenty years: and all the house of Israel lamented after the LORD.

"And Samuel spake unto all the house of Israel, saying, If ye do return unto the LORD with all your hearts, then put away the strange gods and Ashtaroth from among you, and prepare your hearts unto the LORD, and serve him only: and he will deliver you out of the hand of the Philistines.

"Then the children of Israel did put away Baalim and Ashtaroth, and served the LORD only.

"And Samuel said, Gather all Israel to Mizpeh, and I will pray for you unto the LORD.

"And they gathered together to Mizpeh, and drew water, and poured it out before the LORD, and fasted on that day, and said there, We have sinned against the LORD. And Samuel judged the children of Israel in Mizpeh."
          --I Samuel 7:2-6

"And it came to pass, when Ahab heard those words, that he rent his clothes, and put sackcloth upon his flesh, and fasted, and lay in sackcloth, and went softly.

"And the word of the LORD came to Elijah the Tishbite, saying,

"Seest thou how Ahab humbleth himself before me? because he humbleth himself before me, I will not bring the evil in his days: but in his son's days will I bring the evil upon his house."
--I Kings 21:27-29

3. FOR GOD'S PRESENCE.

"Then came to him the disciples of John, saying, Why do we and the Pharisees fast oft, but thy disciples fast not?"   *--Matthew 9:14*

"And the disciples of John and of the Pharisees used to fast: and they come and say unto him, Why do the disciples of John and of the Pharisees fast, but thy disciples fast not?

"And Jesus said unto them, Can the children of the bridechamber fast, while the bridegroom is with them? As long as they have the bridegroom with them, they cannot fast.

"But the days will come, when the bridegroom shall be taken away from them, and then shall they fast in those days." --Mark 2:18-20

"And they said unto him, Why do the disciples of John fast often, and make prayers, and likewise the disciples of the Pharisees; but thine eat and drink?

"And he said unto them, Can ye make the children of the bridechamber fast, while the bridegroom is with them?

"But the days will come, when the bridegroom shall be taken away from them, and then shall they fast in those days." --Luke 5:33-35

4. TO RECEIVE SPIRITUAL DIRECTION.

"Then all the children of Israel, and all the people, went up, and came unto the house of God, and wept, and sat there before the LORD, and fasted that day until even, and offered burnt offerings and peace offerings before the LORD.

"And the children of Israel inquired of the LORD, (for the ark of the covenant of God was there in those days, "And Phinehas, the son of Eleazar, the son of Aaron, stood before it in those days,) saying, Shall I yet again go out to battle against the children of Benjamin my brother, or shall I cease? And the LORD said, Go up; for tomorrow I will deliver them into thine hand."
--Judges 20:26-28

"As they ministered to the Lord, and fasted, the Holy Ghost said, Separate me Barnabas and Saul for the work whereunto I have called them.

"And when they had fasted and prayed, and laid their hands on them, they sent them away." *--Acts 13:2-3*

"And when they had ordained them elders in every church, and had prayed with fasting, they commended them to the Lord, on whom they believed." *--Acts 14:23*

5. SPIRITUAL ENLIGHTENMENT.

"And I set my face unto the Lord God, to seek by prayer and supplications, with fasting, and sackcloth, and ashes:"   *--Daniel 9:3*

"In those days I Daniel was mourning three full weeks.

"I ate no pleasant bread, neither came flesh nor wine in my mouth, neither did I anoint myself at all, till three whole weeks were fulfilled."
--Daniel 10:2-3

"And Cornelius said, Four days ago I was fasting until this hour; and at the ninth hour I prayed in my house, and, behold, a man stood before me in bright clothing,

"And said, Cornelius, thy prayer is heard, and thine alms are had in remembrance in the sight of God.

"Send therefore to Joppa, and call hither Simon, whose surname is Peter; he is lodged in the house of one Simon a tanner by the sea side: who, when he cometh, shall speak unto thee.

"Immediately therefore I sent to thee; and thou hast well done that thou art come. Now therefore are we all here present before God, to hear all things that are commanded thee of God."
--Acts 10:30-33

"Now when much time was spent, and when sailing was now dangerous, because the fast was now already past, Paul admonished them,"
--Acts 27:9

6. AS PART OF OUR CHRISTIAN MINISTRY.

"But in all things approving ourselves as the ministers of God, in much patience, in afflictions, in necessities, in distresses,

"In stripes, in imprisonments, in tumults, in labours, in watchings, in fastings;"

--2 Corinthians 6:4-5

"In weariness and painfulness, in watchings often, in hunger and thirst, in fastings often, in cold and nakedness."

--2 Corinthians 11:27

7. FOR DELIVERANCE FROM DEMONS.

"And when they were come to the multitude, there came to him a certain man, kneeling down to him, and saying, Lord, have mercy on my son: for he is a lunatic, and sore vexed: for ofttimes he falleth into the fire, and oft into the water. And I brought him to thy disciples, and they could not cure him. Then Jesus answered and said, 'O faithless and perverse generation, how long shall I be with you? How long shall I suffer you? Bring him hither to me.' And Jesus rebuked the devil; and he departed out of him: and the child was cured from that very hour." --Matthew 17:14-18

"And when he was come into the house, his disciples asked him privately, Why could not we cast him out? And he said unto them, This kind can come forth by nothing, but by prayer and fasting."

--Mark 9:28-29

-34-

8. TO DELIVER FROM TROUBLE.

"Then the king went to his palace, and passed the night fasting: neither were instruments of music brought before him: and his sleep went from him."
--Daniel 6:18

"And while the day was coming on, Paul besought them all to take meat, saying, This day is the fourteenth day that ye have tarried and continued fasting, having taken nothing.

"Wherefore I pray you to take some meat: for this is for your health: for there shall not an hair fall from the head of any of you."
--Acts 27:33-34

9. FOR FINANCES.

"Blow the trumpet in Zion, sanctify a fast, call a solemn assembly:
"Then will the LORD be jealous for his land, and pity his people.
"Yea, the LORD will answer and say unto his people, Behold, I will send you corn, and wine, and oil, and ye shall be satisfied therewith: and I will no more make you a reproach among the heathen:
" And the floors shall be full of wheat, and the vats shall overflow with wine and oil.
"And I will restore to you the years that the locust hath eaten, the cankerworm, and the caterpillar, and the palmerworm, my great army which I sent among you.

"And ye shall eat in plenty, and be satisfied, and praise the name of the LORD your God, that hath dealt wondrously with you: and my people shall never be ashamed."
--Joel 2:15, 18-19, 24-26

"And Jehoshaphat feared, and set himself to seek the LORD, and proclaimed a fast throughout all Judah."
--2 Chronicles 20:3

"And they rose early in the morning, and went forth into the wilderness of Tekoa: and as they went forth, Jehoshaphat stood and said, Hear me, O Judah, and ye inhabitants of Jerusalem; Believe in the LORD your God, so shall ye be established; believe his prophets, so shall ye prosper."

"And when Jehoshaphat and his people came to take away the spoil of them, they found among them in abundance both riches with the dead bodies, and precious jewels, which they stripped off for themselves, more than they could carry away: and they were three days in gathering of the spoil, it was so much."
--2 Chronicles 20:20, 25

A man came to our city. All he had was in his Studebaker Lark car. He worked, never really made more than $25,000 a year. But he saved some money. He lived very frugally. He also began to fast. He fasted up to 162 days a year. He never fasted any long fasts, but he fasted consistently every week. He began to invest his money into real estate apartments. He eventually began to buy apartment complex after apartment complex. He became one of the most wealthy people I know. He eventually became a very wealthy millionaire.

10. FOR REVIVAL.

"Thus saith the LORD of hosts; The fast of the fourth month, and the fast of the fifth, and the fast of the seventh, and the fast of the tenth, shall be to the house of Judah joy and gladness, and cheerful feasts; therefore love the truth and peace."

--Zechariah 8:19

11. FOR THE SALVATION OF YOUR FAMILY!

To also break generational curses.

"And they that shall be of thee shall build the old waste places: thou shalt raise up the foundations of many generations; and thou shalt be called, The repairer of the breach, The restorer of paths to dwell in."

--Isaiah 58:12

12. FOR MERCY AND GRACE.

We read in the following scripture about God withholding judgment on Ahab, because he humbled himself and fasted.

"And it came to pass, when Ahab heard those words, that he rent his clothes, and put sackcloth upon his flesh, and fasted, and lay in sackcloth, and went softly.

"And the word of the LORD came to Elijah the Tishbite, saying,

"Seest thou how Ahab humbleth himself before me? because he humbleth himself before me, I will not bring the evil in his days: but in his son's days will I bring the evil upon his house."
--I Kings 21:27-29

OLD TESTAMENT:

"And there was set meat before him to eat: but he said, I will not eat, until I have told mine errand. And he said, Speak on."
--Genesis 24:33

"And he was there with the LORD forty days and forty nights; he did neither eat bread, nor drink water. And he wrote upon the tables the words of the covenant, the ten commandments."
--Exodus 34:28

NEW TESTAMENT:

"And when he had fasted forty days and forty nights, he was afterward an hungered."
--Matthew 4:2

"Moreover when ye fast, be not, as the hypocrites, of a sad countenance: for they disfigure their faces, that they may appear unto men to fast. Verily I say unto you, They have their reward. But thou, when thou fastest, anoint thine head, and wash thy face; That thou appear not unto men to fast, but unto thy Father which is in secret: and thy Father, which seeth in secret, shall reward thee openly."   *--Matthew 6:16-18*

CHAPTER 2

DAY 2

DRINKING WATER

Founding Fathers' Prayers Answered
After Much Fasting

A number of years ago my family visited Plymouth, Massachusetts to see the replica of the Mayflower and view Plymouth Rock, the place where the pilgrims first set foot on the New World.

My preconceived ideas of the Pilgrims were old men and women wearing black clothing and long white beards. I was amazed to discover the majority of the Pilgrims were young men and women. For example, William Bradford, the Governor of the colony, was thirty-one years old in 1621 when he took office. Most of the other Pilgrims were about the same age.

Unlike the Puritans who sought reform within the church, the Pilgrims sought liberty themselves. They felt they were on a pilgrimage of truth. They believed the purpose of God was to restore the church to its original condition as shown in the New Testament. They remind me of the Jesus Movement in the 1960's.

With this background, they came to America from

Nottinghamshire, Lincolnshire, and Yorkshire, England. Quoting from Bradford's book, *Of Plymouth Plantation*, they *"joined themselves (by a covenant of the laws) into a church estate, in the fellowship of the gospel . . . for the propagating and advancing of the Gospel of the Kingdom of Christ in the remote parts of the world; yea, though they should be but even as stepping stones unto others for the performing of so great a work."*

Bradford records many answered prayers, which included fasting. One outstanding instance of a public fast was in the summer of 1623.

The Pilgrims' corn crop was in trouble *"by a great drought which continued from the third week in May, 'til about the middle of July without any rain and with great heat for the most part, insomuch as the corn began to wither away. ...It began to languish sore, and some of the drier grounds were parched like withered hay...Upon which we set apart a solemn day of humiliation to seek the Lord by humble and fervent prayer...*

"And He was pleased to give a gracious and speedy answer, both to their own and the Indians' admiration . . . For all the morning and greatest part of the day, it was clear within and very hot, and not a cloud or any sign of rain to be seen; yet toward evening it began to overcast, and shortly after to rain with such sweet and gentle showers as gave them cause of rejoicing and blessing God..."

Usually, if rain falls in such conditions, it comes as thundershowers. This would have destroyed the crops by beating it down. But Bradford relates:

"It came without either wind or thunder or any violence, and by degrees in that abundance as that the earth was thoroughly...soaked therewith. Which did so apparently revive and quicken the decayed corn and other fruits, as was wonderful to see, and made the Indians astonished to behold. And afterwards, the Lord sent them such seasonable showers, with interchange of fair warm weather as, through his blessing, caused a fruitful and liberal harvest."

This practice of setting aside special days of fasting and prayer became an accepted part of life of the Plymouth Colony. On November 15, 1636, a law was passed allowing the Governor and his assistants *"to command solemn days of humiliation by fasting, etc. And, also, for thanksgiving as occasion shall be offered."*

OLD TESTAMENT:

"And this shall be a statute for ever unto you: that in the seventh month, on the tenth day of the month, ye shall afflict your souls, and do no work at all, whether it be one of your own country, or a stranger that sojourneth among you:

"For on that day shall the priest make an atonement for you, to cleanse you, that ye may be clean from all your sins before the LORD.

"It shall be a sabbath of rest unto you, and ye shall afflict your souls, by a statute for ever."
--Leviticus 16:29-31

NEW TESTAMENT:

"Then came to him the disciples of John, saying, Why do we and the Pharisees fast oft, but thy disciples fast not?

And Jesus said unto them, Can the children of the bridechamber mourn, as long as the bridegroom is with them? but the days will come, when the bridegroom shall be taken from them, and then shall they fast."

--Matthew 9:14-15

CHAPTER 3

DAY 3

HOW TO READ THROUGH YOUR BIBLE THIS YEAR!

STRENGTH. Today is your day of strength!
Matthew 11 – 15

> *"Then he said unto them, Go your way, eat the fat, and drink the sweet, and send portions unto them for whom nothing is prepared: for this day is holy unto our Lord: neither be ye sorry; for the joy of the LORD is your strength."*
> *--Nehemiah 8:10*

In the mid-1970's I made a vow to God that never would a day pass that I would not read the Bible. Since that time, I have kept that promise and presently have read the Bible through 35 times.

There is a key scripture I want you to get a hold of. It is Joshua 1:8,

> *"This book of the law shall not depart out of thy mouth; but thou shalt meditate therein day and night, that thou mayest observe to do according to all that is written therein: for then*

thou shalt make thy way prosperous, and then thou shalt have good success."   *--Joshua 1:8*

If a person speaks the word, thinks the word, and ACTS the word, they will be blessed. If you will read the Bible in the morning and at night, you will prosper.

OLD TESTAMENT:

"Also on the tenth day of this seventh month there shall be a day of atonement: it shall be an holy convocation unto you; and ye shall afflict your souls, and offer an offering made by fire unto the LORD."

"It shall be unto you a sabbath of rest, and ye shall afflict your souls: in the ninth day of the month at even, from even unto even, shall ye celebrate your sabbath."

–Leviticus 23:27,32

NEW TESTAMENT:

"Howbeit this kind goeth not out but by prayer and fasting."

--Matthew 17:21

"And the disciples of John and of the Pharisees used to fast: and they come and say unto him, Why do the disciples of John and of the Pharisees fast, but thy disciples fast not?"

--Mark 2:18

CHAPTER 4

DAY 4

A SPECIFIC PLACE FOR FASTING

THERE IS NO WANT. God is meeting all your needs. *Matthew 16 – 20*

> *"The young lions do lack, and suffer hunger: but they that seek the LORD shall not want any good thing."*
> *--Psalm 34:10*

God places great importance on certain places. Jesus instructed 500 people to go to the upper room to tarry for the Holy Spirit's coming. Only 120 obeyed. When Ruth left Moab she came to Bethlehem and met her Boaz. Places really do matter.

Jesus said, *"I must go through Samaria."* Revival broke out when he met the woman at the well in Samaria.

Provisions are assigned places. Elijah was sent to the brook, then to Zarephath. It was there that the widow fed him and sustained him during the famine (I Kings 17).

A husband responds differently to his wife in the bedroom than he does in the workplace. Total honesty is shared. Fears are articulated. Hurts and bruises are exposed so healing can be possible.

The same takes place in prayer. Find a place of solitude to seek God each day.

There are some things you will not pray about if someone else is in the same room. Find a place where you can meet God every day. Let me share five tips for your secret place with God.

1. **HAVE A PLACE WHERE YOU CAN PLAY MUSIC.** Music has great power and can create an atmosphere where God can speak to you. Use a cassette or CD player and play praise music or prayer and meditation music.

   When Elisha needed to hear from God concerning Kings Jehoshaphat and Jehoram, he called for a minstrel. When the minstrel played, the Spirit of God came, and Elisha prophesied deliverance.

2. **KEEP A NOTEBOOK SO YOU CAN DOCUMENT THE WORDS THAT THE HOLY SPIRIT SPEAKS TO YOUR HEART.** If you do not write them down, often you will forget them. When I go to my place of prayer, I always take a tablet and pen so I can write down those things God impresses on my heart.

3. **EXPECT THE HOLY SPIRIT TO MEET YOU IN YOUR SECRET PLACE.** God says,

   "Behold, the days come, saith the LORD, that I

will make a new covenant with the house of Israel,
and with the house of Judah:"

--Jeremiah 31:31

This is God's promise to you. He knows you. He wants to meet you. He wants to communicate His plan for your life.

4. ALLOW GOD TO SPEAK TO YOU THROUGH HIS WORD.

The Word of God is one of the most precious gifts God has given to His church. If you will read the Bible you will see scriptures jump from the pages. These are God's special promises to you. When this happens, memorize those scriptures because God has given them to you. If someone gave you a large sum of money, you would put it in the bank. Well, God has given you something even greater—a promise that can change your life. Deposit that scripture into your spirit as you allow God to speak to you through His Word.

5. THE TIME YOU SPEND IN YOUR SECRET PLACE REVEALS THE AMOUNT OF DESIRE YOU HAVE FOR GOD'S PRESENCE IN YOUR LIFE. Spend time with God. During the time you would ordinarily eat, spend that time in prayer. Your life is never going to be the same, as you seek His presence.

OLD TESTAMENT:

"And ye shall have on the tenth day of this seventh month an holy convocation; and ye shall afflict your souls: ye shall not do any work therein:"

--Numbers 29:7

NEW TESTAMENT:

"And Jesus said unto them, Can the children of the bridechamber fast, while the bridegroom is with them? as long as they have the bridegroom with them, they cannot fast.

"But the days will come, when the bridegroom shall be taken away from them, and then shall they fast in those days."

--Mark 2:19-20

CHAPTER 5

DAY 5

FASTING IN THE SPIRIT

LOVE. You are walking in the love of God and showing it to others! *Matthew 21 – 25*

> *"Love not the world, neither the things that are in the world. If any man love the world, the love of the Father is not in him."*
> *--1 John 2:15*

Most of us find our bodies in open rebellion to the desires of the Spirit. Jesus is the person who said, *"The spirit is willing, but the flesh is weak."* He was speaking to us.

Think of the things that we could do if we would follow Christ in all that we do. If you are anything like me, you become sleepy or distracted within the first minutes of your prayer time.

You want to share your faith, but you become nervous, or feel inadequate, even experiencing fear.

You want to increase your church giving. But you have bills that must be paid.

There was a fellow by the name of Ed. He was a baker in a shopping center. The building owners closed his bakery. They would not renew the lease. He got a job working for his brother, a carpenter. He could only pay him the minimum wage. He was so broke, financially, that all he could afford was ONE light bulb in his house. When he would go into another room, he would unscrew the light bulb, and take it with him into the next room! When Christmas came, he could only afford to buy his wife something that cost 75 cents.

After Christmas he decided he was going to fast. He fasted for one week. During that time, he told God, *"God, since I have been a Christian, I have been a tither. I have honored You. You said You would bless me and rebuke the devourer for my sake."* After he came off his fast, he decided to go over to his bookkeeper and prepare his taxes. His bookkeeper said, *"I have been trying to get a hold of you. There is a baker in town who has two sons, one is a doctor and one is a lawyer---who do not want to carry on the business. He wants to sell four bakeries."*

"You can get in them for $25,000." *"I cannot even afford one light bulb, much less $25,000!"* he said. But as he was driving, he stopped at a traffic light. The Lord spoke to him and said, *"As you fast and pray, you ask me to bless you."* So he turned around and went back to his accountant and told him, *"I am going to try to see if I can get the money and borrow the $25,000."* There were some men in the church that helped him get the $25,000. He bought those bakeries.

God began to prosper him so much that within six months he had paid off that $25,000 loan. The fellow who had not renewed his lease in the other shopping center, called him and said, *"Look, the other tenants we have in there have not worked out."* He gave him free rent to come back and open that bakery again.

When the next Christmas came, God had blessed him so much that his wife bought him an airplane for Christmas.

Believe me---***FASTING WORKS***!

So what are we to do?

There is no one clear answer.

Recall what enticed Adam and Eve . . . that which appeared pleasing. They knew that eating the forbidden fruit was wrong, but it appeared pleasing. Notice how Jesus began His ministry. He rejected that which appeared pleasing; the thought of turning the stones into bread.

Jesus went forty days without food. He overcame any rebellion within himself. He overcame that which appeared pleasing. He did what He knew was best. He followed the Father's will. Through fasting Jesus broke any rebellion that His body might have entertained against Him.

In the same way, when we fast, we take the same stand against sin that Jesus did. Only Jesus' death, burial and resurrection can bring us to salvation.

Through fasting and prayer the Spirit of Christ empowers us to say NO to the devil's ways. Satan has been defeated through the power of the cross. Sin has been overcome. Through fasting and prayer we are able to focus on Christ's redemption, recognizing that his triumph is ours.

The spirit is willing; the flesh will be strengthened.

OLD TESTAMENT:

"Then all the children of Israel, and all the people, went up, and came unto the house of God, and wept, and sat there before the LORD, and fasted that day until even, and offered burnt offerings and peace offerings before the LORD."
--Judges 20:26

"And as he did so year by year, when she went up to the house of the LORD, so she provoked her; therefore she wept, and did not eat.
"Then said Elkanah her husband to her, Hannah, why weepest thou? and why eatest thou not? and why is thy heart grieved? am not I better to thee than ten sons?"
--I Samuel 1:7,8

"And they gathered together to Mizpeh, and drew water, and poured it out before the LORD, and fasted on that day, and said there, We have sinned against the LORD. And Samuel judged the children of Israel in Mizpeh."
--I Samuel 7:6

NEW TESTAMENT:

"And if I send them away fasting to their own houses, they will faint by the way: for divers of them came from far."
--Mark 8:3

CHAPTER 6

DAY 6

FASTING WITH A RIGHT HEART!

VICTORY. Today your promise is a day of total victory! Do not settle for less!   *Matthew 26 – 28*

> *"No weapon that is formed against thee shall prosper; and every tongue that shall rise against thee in judgment thou shalt condemn. This is the heritage of the servants of the LORD, and their righteousness is of me, saith the LORD."*
> *--Isaiah 54:17*

> *"When a man's ways please the LORD, he maketh even his enemies to be at peace with him."*
> *--Proverbs 16:7*

I once met a man who was very bitter. He was resentful of others. As he fasted he prayed for God's judgment on those with whom he didn't agree. He developed a spirit of anger, resentment, and a *"get-even attitude."* No one liked being around him. The fruit of the Spirit was not evident in his life.

This man fasted but his heart was not right. This

opened the door for evil spirits to get control. They eventually destroyed him. Unlike this man, you need to ask God to take all bitterness and resentment from you.

To love God and to love others is our goal. Fasting and prayer heightens our recognition of God in our life. As a result we recognize our need to love others.

Fasting is not an end in itself. It is intended to cultivate a greater closeness to God. Then we can become clearer channels of His Spirit and develop godliness in all of our relationships. Those are the results we desire; those are the results God desires.

As we discipline our desires, we can become more responsive to the needs of others, especially the hungry and the poor.

OLD TESTAMENT:
> *"So David hid himself in the field: and when the new moon was come, the king sat him down to eat meat."*
>
> *--I Samuel 20:24*

CHAPTER 7

DAY 7

HUNGERING AND THIRSTING AFTER RIGHTEOUSNESS

DIRECTION. God is showing you direction and what to do!   *Mark 1 – 5*

> *"I would lead thee, and bring thee into my mother's house, who would instruct me: I would cause thee to drink of spiced wine of the juice of my pomegranate."*   *--Song of Solomon 8:2*

> *"Thou art snared with the words of thy mouth, thou art taken with the words of thy mouth."*   *--Proverbs 6:22*

When Jesus was baptized by John in the River Jordan, immediately He was led into the wilderness.

> *"Then was Jesus led up of the Spirit into the wilderness to be tempted of the devil."*
> *--Matthew 4:1*

In Mark 1:12, He was driven into the wilderness.

> *"And immediately the Spirit driveth him into the wilderness."*   *--Mark 1:12*

-55-

He was both driven and led to an encounter with the Holy Spirit. There He fasted for 40 days. During this time He drank plenty of liquids. After His 40-day fast, the Gospels state that Jesus began to perform miracles. Jesus said,

> *"Verily, verily, I say unto you, He that believeth on me, the works that I do shall he do also; and greater works than these shall he do; because I go unto my Father."*   *--John 14:12*

Later the Spirit prompted Paul to write,

> *"But covet earnestly the best gifts: and yet show I unto you a more excellent way."*
> *--1 Corinthians 12:31*

The question is, how did Jesus eagerly desire spiritual gifts? Did He just wish for them? Did He just think how wonderful it would be to have them?

No! The way Jesus desired spiritual gifts was through fasting. He did not perform any miracles until after he fasted for 40 days!

When I pastored in Lexington, Kentucky, I began to fast a day a week for five years. I was so hungry for God to empower me that I began to fast three days at a time without food or water.

I remember a cold January when I had not eaten or drunk water in three days. When I went to church that evening on the third day, God spoke to me through a word of knowledge.

I said, *"There is a woman here who is deaf."* As I looked over the small congregation, I realized I knew everyone who was there. I could not believe what I just said. As far as I knew, no one was deaf.

I began to pray, *"Lord, why didn't You speak to me about a headache or a backache. I don't believe anyone is deaf."*

No one responded. Finally, a woman came forward who wanted prayer for her husband. When I started to pray for her, I noticed she was wearing two hearing aids. She had been deaf since she was two years old! After prayer, she could hear the tick of a watch. She was totally healed!

During the next few days of the fast, I encourage you to pray specifically for God to give you the best gifts. I encourage you to pray for gifts that will encourage others, heal others, and bring others into the Kingdom.

OLD TESTAMENT:
> *"And they found an Egyptian in the field, and brought him to David, and gave him bread, and he did eat; and they made him drink water;*
> *"And they gave him a piece of a cake of figs, and two clusters of raisins: and when he had eaten, his spirit came again to him: for he had eaten no bread, nor drunk any water, three days and three nights."* **--I Samuel 30:11,12**

NEW TESTAMENT:
> *"And she was a widow of about fourscore and four years, which departed not from the temple, but served God with fastings and prayers night and day."*
> **--Luke 2:37**

CHAPTER 8

DAY 8

FASTING LAUNCHES MINISTRY

FAMILY. Good things are going to happen to your family! *Mark 6 – 10*

> *"Wealth and riches shall be in his house: and his righteousness endureth for ever."*
> *--Psalm 112:1-3*

> *"And all thy children shall be taught of the Lord; and great shall be the peace of thy children."*
> *--Isaiah 54:13*

Did you know that the apostle Paul's ministry began during a corporate fast in his church? The church at Antioch was praying for direction. How were they to further the Kingdom of God?

> *"As they ministered to the Lord, and fasted, the Holy Ghost said, Separate me Barnabas and Saul for the work whereunto I have called them."*
> *--Acts 13:2*

Thereafter, Barnabas and Saul set out on missionary adventures that changed the shape of Christianity. Further it changed the shape of the western world. Christianity eventually replaced the pagan practices of the Roman Empire.

Many people assume that Saul changed his name as a result of his encounter with Christ on the Damascus road. That is not the case. Saul changed his name to Paul shortly after Barnabas and he became missionaries.

"Then Saul, (who also is called Paul,) filled with the Holy Ghost, set his eyes on him,"
--Acts 13:9

As a result of prayer and fasting, Paul changed his name and changed his mission in life.

What can we learn from the church in Antioch?

FIRST, the church at Antioch practiced corporate prayer and fasting. Paul and Barnabas were called into ministry during the midst of one of these fasts.

SECOND, the church at Antioch was sensitive to the works of the Spirit. The Holy Spirit called Paul and Barnabas into ministry. The Spirit spoke in the gift of prophecy through members in the church and confirmed that prophecy in the church.

THIRD, the church at Antioch was a church of action. Having learned the will of God, they acted.

OLD TESTAMENT:

"And they mourned, and wept, and fasted until even, for Saul, and for Jonathan his son, and for the people of the LORD, and for the house of Israel; because they were fallen by the sword."

--II Samuel 1:12

"And when all the people came to cause David to eat meat while it was yet day, David sware, saying, So do God to me, and more also, if I taste bread, or ought else, till the sun be down."

--II Samuel 3:35

NEW TESTAMENT:

"And they said unto him, Why do the disciples of John fast often, and make prayers, and likewise the disciples of the Pharisees; but thine eat and drink?

"And he said unto them, Can ye make the children of the bridechamber fast, while the bridegroom is with them?"

--Luke 5:33-35

"For John the Baptist came neither eating bread nor drinking wine; and ye say, He hath a devil."

--Luke 7:33

CHAPTER 9

DAY 9

EXPECT GOD'S PLAN FOR YOUR FUTURE

FAITH. Walk in God's faith and power!
Mark 11 – 16

> *"Whereby are given unto us exceeding great and precious promises: that by these ye might be partakers of the divine nature, having escaped the corruption that is in the world through lust."*
>
> *--2 Peter 1:4*

The greatest promises in the Bible are in Isaiah 58. It is the fasting chapter.

> *"And the LORD shall guide thee continually, and satisfy thy soul in drought, and make fat thy bones: and thou shalt be like a watered garden, and like a spring of water, whose waters fail not."*
>
> *--Isaiah 58:11*

God promises His guidance and direction to people who fast.

Years ago I was flying a little airplane. I was apprehensive, because I was lost. Finally I found a little town where there was a small airport. When I landed, the friend who was with me said, *"I'm going to ask somebody where we are."*

"No," I said. *"They will know we are lost. Just ask to use the phone book, and that will tell us where we are."*

These 21 days of prayer and fasting can bring God's focus into your life. You can find out the right road and mission for yourself.

Today, there are three specific areas I want you to seek God for in your life:

1. GOD WILL GUIDE YOU IN YOUR FINANCES.

"Then shall thy light break forth as the morning,and thine health shall spring forth speedily: and thy righteousness shall go before thee; the glory of the LORD shall be thy reward."
--Isaiah 58:8

God wants you to be blessed in your finances.

"The LORD is my shepherd; I shall not want."
--Psalm 23:1

"Let them shout for joy, and be glad, that favour my righteous cause: yea, let them say continually, Let the LORD be magnified, which

hath pleasure in the prosperity of his servant."
--Psalm 35:27

"The young lions do lack, and suffer hunger: but they that seek the LORD shall not want any good thing."
--Psalm 34:10

The largest givers in our church are people who fast. In no way do I want to imply that the more money you have, the more spiritual you are. I have known people who were very wealthy, and yet were very carnal in their relationship to spiritual things. On the other hand, I have known very godly people who did not have much money.

However, one of the first things that fasting does in a person's life is to break poverty and debt. If you will have a lifestyle of fasting, you will begin to see prosperity come to you. This is not saying that if you fast one time you are going to be rich. But, if you fast continually, God will bless you financially in a way you have never dreamed.

2. GOD HAS A PLAN FOR YOUR FAMILY.

Luke 15 tells about three things that were lost. One was a shepherd who had 99 sheep, but lost one. Second, there is a story about a lady who lost a coin in her home. The third is the story of the prodigal son who left home. In each of these stories, that which was lost was found. The shepherd found his lost sheep. The lady found the lost coin, and the prodigal son came home.

Jesus is declaring that none will be lost. None of your family will be lost to the devil as we stand in the gap.

Not one husband, not one son, not one daughter, none of your family has to go to hell.

I believe God is sending a great revival that is going to touch every family and every home.

> *"And they that shall be of thee shall build the old waste places: thou shalt raise up the foundations of many generations; and thou shalt be called, The repairer of the breach, The restorer of paths to dwell in."*
> *--Isaiah 58:12*

God will help you raise up a family not under the curse of the devil, but under the blessing of God.

3. EXPECT GOD'S PLAN FOR YOUR FUTURE.

Did you know that you have an assignment in life?

a. Everything that God has made was created to solve an existing problem. God has made you to be the answer to some situation in life.

b. Most people never discover their true assignment and mission in life. However, that person does not have to be you.

> *"Wherefore be ye not unwise, but understanding what the will of the Lord is."*
> *--Ephesians 5:17*

c. Every assignment has a birthplace. Let this 21 day fast be the birthplace where you find your true mission in life.

OLD TESTAMENT: *I Kings 13:8-24*

"And he arose, and did eat and drink, and went in the strength of that meat forty days and forty nights unto Horeb the mount of God."
--I Kings 19:8

NEW TESTAMENT:
"I fast twice in the week, I give tithes of all that I possess."
--Luke 18:12

CHAPTER 10

DAY 10

THE RIGHT REASON TO FAST

GOD'S WILL IN MY LIFE. Declare God's will in every situation!   *Luke 1 – 5*

Isaiah 58 is the chapter in the Bible that tells about fasting. Hebrews 11 talks of faith. I Corinthians 13 talks about love. Notice how Isaiah 58 begins,

"'Why have we fasted' they say, and You have not seen?

Why have we afflicted our souls, and You take no notice?

Indeed you fast for strife and debate. And to strike with the fist of wickedness.... Is it a fast that I have chosen, A day for a man to afflict his soul?...

Is this not the fast that I have chosen: To loose the bonds of wickedness, To undo the heavy burdens, To let the oppressed go free, And that you break every yoke?" (Isaiah 58:1-6 NKJV)

Gordon Cove, **Revival Now Through Prayer and Fasting**, notes that God, through the prophet Isaiah, instructs His people about a right reason and a wrong reason to fast.

"Having shown them where they were wrong, He proceeds to give them instructions and promises regarding the right way to fast. So that all the promises mentioned here are conditional upon us exercising the correct method of fasting. These promises begin at verse eight."

Then your light shall break forth speedily, And your righteousness shall go before you; The glory of the Lord shall be your rear guard."

--Isaiah 58:8

Gordon Cove continues, *"The first word of the verse is 'Then.' This means, 'at that time,' or, 'after something else has happened.' It is only when we are practicing the fast that God has chosen, that we can claim the promise. Not until then."*

OLD TESTAMENT:

"And Ahab came into his house heavy and displeased because of the word which Naboth the Jezreelite had spoken to him: for he had said, I will not give thee the inheritance of my fathers. And he laid him down upon his bed, and turned away his face, and would eat no bread.

"But Jezebel his wife came to him, and said unto him, Why is thy spirit so sad, that thou eatest no bread?"

--I Kings 21:4,5

"And she wrote in the letters, saying, Proclaim a fast, and set Naboth on high among the people:

"They proclaimed a fast, and set Naboth on high among the people."
--I Kings 21:9,12

"And it came to pass, when Ahab heard those words, that he rent his clothes, and put sackcloth upon his flesh, and fasted, and lay in sackcloth, and went softly."
--I Kings 21:27

NEW TESTAMENT:

"And he was three days without sight, and neither did eat nor drink."
--Acts 9:9

CHAPTER 11

DAY 11

THE PROMISES OF
A RIGHT FAST

Yesterday, we considered what is the right way to fast. Today, we receive the promises of a right fast. We again look at the writing of Gordon Cove, who comments on Isaiah 58, verse 8.

"The first promise is: 'Then shall thy light break forth as the morning.' This is a promise of illumination. For light to break forth as the morning, must be an obvious reference to the dawn of a new day. Thus the promise offers us a new dawn of spiritual illumination, if we betake ourselves to fasting. Anyone who has practiced fasting for periods, will tell you that after so many days the mind takes on a new clarity of thought…The Bible becomes lit up with a new beauty…

"'Thine health shall spring forth speedily.' Someone must say, 'Does this mean spiritual or physical health?' It must surely include both. After fasting, your spiritual health will be greater than before. Things will have dropped off your soul during the fast. But the Scriptures also teach that it is the will of God that we should 'prosper and be in health (bodily), even as thy soul prospereth' (III John 2). Many people have been healed of long-standing complaints while fasting. So fasting can help you to health!...

"'Thy righteousness shall go before thee.' This means your life after fasting will have more influence for Jesus and will carry more weight for God than before. In other words, others will see Jesus in you. One of the great hindrances to the march of Christianity is the inconsistencies of Christians. Fasting will help you get rid of these and therefore your spiritual influence will go out from now on in ever-widening circles."

OLD TESTAMENT:
> *"They arose, all the valiant men, and took away the body of Saul, and the bodies of his sons, and brought them to Jabesh, and buried their bones under the oak in Jabesh, and fasted seven days."* --I Chronicles 10:12

> *"And Jehoshaphat feared, and set himself to seek the LORD, and proclaimed a fast throughout all Judah."* --II Chronicles 20:3

NEW TESTAMENT:
> *"And Cornelius said, Four days ago I was fasting until this hour; and at the ninth hour I prayed in my house, and, behold, a man stood before me in bright clothing,"*
> --Acts 10:30

CHAPTER 12

DAY 12

FASTING MUST INCLUDE GOD'S WORD

THE LORD WILL ANSWER YOUR PRAYER!

Have you ever felt that God was not answering your prayers? Have you felt that your cries were going unheard? In reflecting upon Isaiah 58, Gordon Cove lists ten benefits of fasting. We have considered three of those benefits.

(4) "The glory of the Lord will be thy rereward." This word "rereward" has been interpreted as "The Backer-up." The glory of God will follow us wherever we go. Your influence will go before you, and the glory of God will be your rear-guard . . . When you have fasted, unspeakable glory will rest upon you.

(5) "Then shalt thou call, and the Lord shall answer; thou shalt cry, and He shall say, 'Here I am.' " Here is a wonderful promise that, having fasted, your prayers will be answered speedily. The longer you fast, the greater the answers will be to your prayers. Fasting smashes any hesitancy on God's part to answer, for He sees that you now mean business!...

(6) "Then shall thy light rise in obscurity, and thy darkness as the noon day." No matter how dark the night, your light will go on shining for God. The darker the night, the brighter it will shine. Have you ever been lost at night in the country, where, perhaps, you could not see your own hand before you? How glad you felt when at last you suddenly spied a light in the distance. Perhaps it was only a light from a small lamp, but your heart almost leaped for joy as you made your way towards it. So also there will be many hearts that leap for joy when you have fasted, and as you see your light shining for God...

(7) "And the Lord shall guide thee continually." After fasting comes guidance. No doubt one of the greatest problems of all Christians is to be able to discern the spirits, and to know whether it is God leading them, or whether some evil spirit is trying to sidetrack them. According to this promise, God has bound Himself, if we meet the condition of fasting, to guide us continually.

OLD TESTAMENT:

"And at the evening sacrifice I arose up from my heaviness; and having rent my garment and my mantle, I fell upon my knees, and spread out my hands unto the LORD my God,"
--Ezra 9:5

"Then Ezra rose up from before the house of God, and went into the chamber of Johanan the son of Eliashib: and when he came thither, he did eat no bread, nor drink water: for he mourned because of the transgression of them that had been carried away."
--Ezra 10:6

"And it came to pass, when I heard these words, that I sat down and wept, and mourned certain days, and fasted, and prayed before the God of heaven,"

--Nehemiah 1:4

"Now in the twenty and fourth day of this month the children of Israel were assembled with fasting, and with sackclothes, and earth upon them."   *--Nehemiah 9:1*

NEW TESTAMENT:

"As they ministered to the Lord, and fasted, the Holy Ghost said, Separate me Barnabas and Saul for the work whereunto I have called them."

--Acts 13:2,3

The 21-Day Fast

CHAPTER 13

DAY 13

HEALTH BENEFITS

GOOD THINGS. God gives good things to your life! *Luke 16 – 20*

"For the LORD God is a sun and shield: the LORD will give grace and glory: no good thing will he withhold from them that walk uprightly." --Psalm 84:11

A 77-year-old physician fasted for 53 days. Dr. Henry S. Tanner, a medical doctor in the 1880's, sought to prove fasting could improve a person's health. At that time doctors and theologians ridiculed him, not believing that he could survive a 40-day fast like Moses or Jesus.

At the age of 50, under strict supervision, Dr. Tanner fasted for 43 days without food. The newspapers covered the story. At the conclusion of this fast he claimed to have seen heaven, angels, and the Lord Jesus Christ. Tanner became a pioneer for the advancement of fasting. He taught it and prescribed it to his patients. At age 60, he fasted for 50 days.

In the middle of this fast he *saw "the unspeakable glories of God."* He came out of that fast feeling 30 years younger. He looked like he was only 40 years old.

At age 77, Dr. Tanner fasted for 53 days. Dr. Tanner's gray hair was replaced by new black hair. It was the same color that it was when he was a young man. He died at the age of 93.

OLD TESTAMENT:

"Go, gather together all the Jews that are present in Shushan, and fast ye for me, and neither eat nor drink three days, night or day: I also and my maidens will fast likewise; and so will I go in unto the king, which is not according to the law: and if I perish, I perish."

--Esther 4:16

"Then said Esther, If it please the king, let it be granted to the Jews which are in Shushan to do tomorrow also according unto this day's decree, and let Haman's ten sons be hanged upon the gallows."

--Esther 9:13

"He is chastened also with pain upon his bed, and the multitude of his bones with strong pain: So that his life abhorreth bread, and his soul dainty meat."

--Job 33:19,20

"But as for me, when they were sick, my clothing was sackcloth: I humbled my soul with fasting; and my prayer returned into mine own bosom."

--Psalm 35:13

NEW TESTAMENT:
> *"And when they had ordained them elders in every church, and had prayed with fasting, they commended them to the Lord, on whom they believed."*   *--Acts 14:23*

God can heal you if you fast!

Once while I was fasting 21 days, I was called to the hospital to pray for a man who was brain dead. He had been on life supports for two weeks, with no brain activity at all. I went in and prayed for this man. Then the doctors proceeded to turn off all of his life support. They took the ventilator out of his lungs and said, *"Now, he is going to die!"* I was there with his son, the wife and the children. But he continued to breathe.

Finally, they put him in a room. After two hours he rose from the bed and said to his son, *"How long have I been out?"* God totally healed him and raised him up. He later worked with me on my staff as a hospital visitation pastor.

I had been fasting for a number of days. While I was praying God spoke to me to get up and go to the hospital and pray for a man. So I got up and drove straight to the hospital. It was about 11:30 p.m. I walked into this man's room. A nurse walked in and said, *"Are you a member of the family? You are the first to arrive. We have tried to call…"* I said, *"No, I am his pastor."*

She said, *"He is dying; if he is not dead already. We were trying to call the family to tell them to come."* So I began to pray for him and he opened his eyes. He said,

"Well, pastor, have you seen the angels? I've been to heaven." As we were talking, strength came back to him. He sat up straight in his bed. He was alert as anybody could be. His sons, daughter and wife soon came in. They expected to see him dead. There he was, healthier than he had been in years. He said, *"Well, my greatest desire is to see my family come to the Lord."* None of his kids were saved. So we joined hands and prayed together. Every one of his kids came to Christ. He got so strong, that in two days they released him from the hospital to go home.

He was home for about a month. There had been some hurts in the family; all of that was healed. After about a month, he told his wife, *"You know, I just don't feel well today, can you take me to the hospital?"* She drove him to the hospital. He laid down, closed his eyes, and went to heaven. He died the most peaceful death; and all of his family came to the Lord.

God had spoken to me while I was fasting. He told me to go to the hospital.

CHAPTER 14

DAY 14

MAN DOES NOT LIVE
BY BREAD ALONE

PEACE. Speak words of peace to your problems!
Luke 21 – 24

"Thou wilt keep him in perfect peace, whose mind is stayed on thee: because he trusteth in thee."   *--Isaiah 26:3*

"Therefore being justified by faith, we have peace with God through our Lord Jesus Christ:"   *--Romans 5:1*

When was the last time you were tempted to take the easy way out? Perhaps last month...last week... yesterday...five minutes ago?

Every day we make numerous decisions. Only a few of those decisions are life-changing by themselves. Yet together they establish a way of living. They become part of your discipline of life.

The discipline of Jesus can be summarized in two commandments: Loving God and loving people.

"This is the first and great commandment."
--Matthew 22:38

This sounds good. The golden rule is even based upon the second of these commandments.

But how did Jesus put these into action?

How do we put these commandments into practice?

Let's look to the life of Jesus for clues.

1. JESUS PUBLICLY DECLARED HIS LOVE FOR THE FATHER.

The first public declaration by Jesus of His love for the Father was His baptism. Jesus publicly declared His love for the Father many times. But we look to His baptism as a focal point. Baptism is your focal point. While it may not have been the point where you made a personal commitment to Christ, it is your public declaration. You can always look back and say, *"There is where I started."*

2. JESUS EXPRESSED HIS LOVE FOR THE FATHER PRIVATELY.

Immediately after His baptism Jesus was led into the desert where Jesus' love for His Father was tested. When you make public declarations, you will be tested. Are your commitments for show, or are they for real?

Jesus expressed His love for the Father through 40 days of fasting and prayer. During this time, Jesus was tested three times.

FIRST....the devil said, *"Tell this stone to become bread."*

Let's look at three scriptures in Luke, chapter 4:

> *"And Jesus answered him, saying, It is written, That man shall not live by bread alone, but by every word of God."*
> *--Luke 4:4*

> *"And Jesus answered and said unto him, Get thee behind me, Satan: for it is written, Thou shalt worship the Lord thy God, and him only shalt thou serve."*
> *--Luke 4:8*

> *"And Jesus answering said unto him, It is said, Thou shalt not tempt the Lord thy God."*
> *--Luke 4:12*

Jesus knew that the most important things in life are not what we have. They are who we are. We are the children of the Father. As children of the Father, we place our trust in Him.

SECOND....Jesus was tested to take authority over the world. But Jesus' authority lay in the hands of the Father.

Often we think we must control everything in our life. Some things are beyond our control. You have one thing you can always control; that is your commitment to Christ. When your commitment to Christ is expressed in a disciplined manner, the other areas of your life will fall into place. You will express your discipleship in expressions of love for God and expressions of love for others. Fasting and prayer focuses that commitment.

THIRD...Jesus was tempted to use miracles in a magical way. He was to throw Himself from the height of a high point and let the angels catch Him.

The giftings and miracles of the Spirit are to strengthen your commitment to Christ and to express God's love to others. Jesus left the desert empowered by the Spirit for service. During these days of fasting and prayer, let us pray that the Spirit helps us to develop our love for God and our love for others.

OLD TESTAMENT:

"And in every province, whithersoever the king's commandment and his decree came, there was great mourning among the Jews, and fasting, and weeping, and wailing; and many lay in sackcloth and ashes."   *--Esther 4:3*

"When I wept, and chastened my soul with fasting, that was to my reproach."   *--Psalm 69:10*

"My heart is smitten, and withered like grass; so that I forget to eat my bread."
                                    --Psalm 102:4

"Fools because of their transgression, and because of their iniquities, are afflicted.
"Their soul abhorreth all manner of meat; and they draw near unto the gates of death."
                              -- Psalm 107:17,18

NEW TESTAMENT:

"And when it was day, certain of the Jews banded together, and bound themselves under a curse, saying that they would neither eat nor drink till they had killed Paul. And they were more than forty which had made this conspiracy. And they came to the chief priests and elders, and said, We have bound ourselves under a great curse, that we will eat nothing until we have slain Paul. Now therefore ye with the council signify to the chief captain that he bring him down unto you to morrow, as though ye would inquire something more perfectly concerning him: and we, or ever he come near, are ready to kill him. And when Paul's sister's son heard of their lying in wait, he went and entered into the castle, and told Paul. Then Paul called one of the centurions unto him, and said, Bring this young man unto the chief captain: for he hath a certain thing to tell him. So he took him, and brought him to the chief captain, and said, Paul the prisoner called me unto him, and prayed me to bring this young man unto thee, who hath something to say unto thee. Then the chief captain took him by the hand, and went with him aside privately, and asked him, What is that thou hast to tell me? And he said, The Jews have agreed to desire thee that thou wouldest bring down Paul to morrow into the council, as though they would inquire somewhat of him more perfectly. But do not thou yield unto them: for there lie in wait for him of them more than forty men, which have bound themselves with an oath, that they will neither eat nor drink till they have killed him: and now are they ready, looking for a promise from thee."

--Acts 23:12-21

CHAPTER 15

DAY 15

FASTING AS A LIFESTYLE

DESIRES ARE MET.   Your desires are being met
through God's blessings!

John 1 – 4

During these 21 days you will be praying that your
desires would be the desires of God; that God's will for
your life would be reflected in your desires.

After the fast, expect God to give you the desires of
your heart.

I would like you to consider making prayer and
fasting a normal part of your life.

During the 1800's our nation was brought to its
knees through numerous revivals which spread throughout
the states west of the Appalachian Mountains. The most
notable of these revivals erupted at Cane Ridge, Kentucky.

Prior to these revivals, few people attended church.
Few followed Christ. Kentucky was considered the state
farthest away from God.   There was more violence,
fighting, and alcoholism than in most states. A group of

pastors banded together to fast and pray. As a result of the revivals, churches dotted the landscape, slavery was abolished, and women were given opportunities to preach and participate in their communities.

How did these revivals begin?

They began with prayer and fasting.

The leading figure in these revivals was Francis Asbury, the Methodist bishop. Following John Wesley's lead, Asbury and Methodist circuit riding preachers fasted twice a week.

Revival resulted as ordinary people prayed, fasted and took action.

Will you join me in making prayer and fasting a lifestyle?

You may choose to fast twice a week. You may choose to set aside a three-day period each month.

Together, we will change the face of our city, America and the world.

> *"If my people, which are called by my name, shall humble themselves, and pray, and seek my face, and turn from their wicked ways; then will I hear from heaven, and will forgive their sin, and will heal their land."*
> *--2 Chronicles 7:14*

OLD TESTAMENT:

"My knees are weak through fasting; and my flesh faileth of fatness."
--Psalm 109:24

"Therefore go thou, and read in the roll, which thou hast written from my mouth, the words of the LORD in the ears of the people in the LORD'S house upon the fasting day: and also thou shalt read them in the ears of all Judah that come out of their cities.
"And it came to pass in the fifth year of Jehoiakim the son of Josiah king of Judah, in the ninth month, that they proclaimed a fast before the LORD to all the people in Jerusalem, and to all the people that came from the cities of Judah unto Jerusalem." *--Jeremiah 36:6,9*

Daniel 1:12-16

"Then the king went to his palace, and passed the night fasting: neither were instruments of music brought before him: and his sleep went from him."
--Daniel 6:18

"And I set my face unto the Lord God, to seek by prayer and supplications, with fasting, and sackcloth, and ashes:"
--Daniel 9:3

NEW TESTAMENT:

> *"Defraud ye not one the other, except it be with consent for a time, that ye may give yourselves to fasting and prayer; and come together again, that Satan tempt you not for your incontinency."*
>
> *--I Corinthians 7:5*

CHAPTER 16

DAY 16

FASTING TO BREAK STRONGHOLDS

CURSES ARE BROKEN. All generation curses are broken! *John 5 – 8*

> *"Christ hath redeemed us from the curse of the law, being made a curse for us: for it is written, Cursed is every one that hangeth on a tree:"*
> *--Galatians 3:13*

Fasting multiplies the effect of prayer at least several times. Fasting will touch things that prayer alone cannot break.

When God's people humbled themselves in prayer and fasting, he responds. His purposes will be accomplished in situations that look hopeless.

The people of Judah faced extermination when the Moabites and the Ammorites warred against them. Judah was paying the consequences of her sin against God. They had set up idols and looked to them instead of their creator. But, when King Jehoshaphat heard of the coming attack, he inquired of the Lord.

He proclaimed a fast. The people of Judah united together to seek deliverance from their enemy by looking to their God.

They humbled themselves and said,

> *"O our God, wilt thou not judge them? for we have no might against this great company that cometh against us; neither know we what to do: but our eyes are upon thee."*
> *--2 Chronicles 20:12*

God answered their prayers in such a powerful way that fear came upon all of the surrounding nations. They turned away from their sins. They prayed and fasted. God heard them.

He answered them, provided for them, and delivered them from their enemy. God empowered them with what was needed for victory in their circumstances.

Each of us needs to take inventory of our lives. What are the strongholds that keep us from receiving answers to our prayers? The Holy Spirit will convict us of sin in our lives. We need to listen. Once those areas are revealed, we need to turn away from them so that they are not threaded into the fabric of our being.

The same process needs to happen in the areas of our family, our relationships, our work, and our nation.

We need to let go of our own notions and take hold of God's way. Just like the people of Judah we can turn away from our sins and look to God with our whole heart.

Prayer should be coupled with fasting. Together these disciples help us deny our own way and look to God for his strength and direction.

We are in a spiritual battle between the forces of heaven and hell.

Be willing to deny your physical desires to humbly and earnestly seek the face of God. Prayer coupled with times of fasting will bring new strength to you and tear down the strongholds in your life; strongholds which have been set up to keep you from the blessings of God.

Once I had been fasting for three days. I was driving in an affluent part of town, when suddenly in front of my car passed what appeared to be a huge deer. It went across the road and right into a house. I pulled the car over. I began to pray, *"Lord, what was that?"* The Lord showed me. It was the strongman that ruled that part of our city. God also showed me it was a spirit of lust that was the controlling power in that area of our community. As you fast, the spiritual world begins to be opened and unlocked unto you.

God wants you to overcome the strongholds of life. He will win the battle for you as you humble yourself. Begin with prayer, coupled with times of fasting.

For over 25 years, I have consistently fasted at least one day a week. As you do, it really puts you on the cutting edge, spiritually. It makes you sensitive to spiritual things. One night at midnight, my dogs began to bark. My wife said, *"Go down and check on the dogs."* I went out and checked on the dogs. As I walked past the garage, there was a huge angel standing beside the garage.

When I got back to bed, I said, *"Margaret, there was an angel."* She said, *"Well, what did he want?"* I said, *"I don't know."* I begin to pray and read the Bible. After about 30 minutes I had come to the conclusion that it was a Guardian Angel above our house.

Another time around 12:30 in the morning, the doorbell rang, so I went downstairs. This fellow was standing at the door, said, *"My car has broken down. Can I come in and make a phone call?"* Ordinarily, I would have probably let him come in. But I felt I had been warned by an angel. I told him, *"No, my family is asleep. But I will be glad to make a call for you. What number is it?"* He gave me a number and I called it. But when I looked outside I never saw his car broken down. I think he had probably come to do me harm. He disappeared from the front porch. But I had been warned. It was while I was fasting on a 24-hour fast.

Through fasting, you can take **SPIRITUAL AUTHORITY!**

A friend of mine developed a growth on his ear. He went to this doctor in his church. The doctor said, *"Pastor, I want you to go see a specialist, that could be cancer."* So he went to the specialist. It was diagnosed as fast-spreading melanoma. The doctor urged, *"If we do not operate immediately and take some of this ear off, you could die."* He told the doctor, *"Well, before I do that, I feel like I should fast and pray."* He went on a 40-day fast.

While he was on this fast, he was asked to come and pray for a woman who was bedridden. He went into the room where her husband was kneeling on the other side of the bed. She was lying there, bound by demons. From her position, she couldn't see this growth on his ear. Without even looking at him, these demons spoke out of her and said, *"Hugh"*. She laughed a blood-curdling laugh. The demons said, *"Do you expect to get the demons out of me, when you cannot even get yourself healed of cancer of the ear."* She laughed again.

It made him so angry, he turned and walked out of the room; and walked into the bathroom of this house. He said, *"You foul devil, you will not destroy me with cancer."* He reached up and grabbed this melanoma on his ear and jerked it right off his ear. The blood began to go everywhere. He washed himself and got a towel. It finally stopped bleeding. He walked back and cast the demons out of that woman and she was totally healed.

He went back home. The next Sunday he was in church, and this same doctor came up and said, *"Oh pastor, let me see that ear. That operation that the doctor did was a good operation. That thing looks like you had never had cancer before."*

He never told that doctor what had happened. But God had totally healed him during that 40-day fast.

OLD TESTAMENT:
>*"In those days I Daniel was mourning three full weeks.*
>*"I ate no pleasant bread, neither came flesh nor wine in my mouth, neither did I anoint myself at all, till three whole weeks were fulfilled."*
>   *--Daniel 10:2,3*

"Sanctify ye a fast, call a solemn assembly, gather the elders and all the inhabitants of the land into the house of the LORD your God, and cry unto the LORD."

--Joel 1:14

"Therefore also now, saith the LORD, turn ye even to me with all your heart, and with fasting, and with weeping, and with mourning:"

--Joel 2:12

"Blow the trumpet in Zion, sanctify a fast, call a solemn assembly:"

--Joel 2:15

CHAPTER 17

DAY 17

FASTING FOR YOUR CITY
PRAYER WALKING

NEEDS ARE MET. Depend upon God to meet all your needs! *John 9 – 12*

> *"But my God shall supply all your need according to his riches in glory by Christ Jesus."*
> *--Philippians 4:19*

For six days the Hebrew people walked around the city of Jericho. On the seventh day God delivered the city (Joshua 6). The city had been promised to be delivered to Israel. They were asked to do one thing. They were to walk around the city, praying for seven days.

God is going to deliver our city. During our fast, I walked around our city. Scores of prayer warriors joined me as I literally walked 91 miles around the City of Louisville. We surrounded our city with prayer and fasting. We walked around the walls of unbelief, poverty, racism, laziness, and social elitism. Those walls are starting to tumble down.

In hundreds of cities across the globe, ordinary believers are *"prayer walking"* through the streets of their communities. Prayer walking is *"praying on-site with insight."* There is no set pattern or proven formula.

Prayer walkers have set out with every imaginable style. There is nothing magical in the footsteps. God's Spirit is helping us to pray with persistence in the midst of the very settings in which we expect him to answer our prayers. We instinctively draw near to those for whom we pray.

CHOOSE AN AREA. Praying over your neighborhood will prepare your neighbors to receive your invitation to your group. Getting up close to the community focuses our prayer. We sharpen our prayers by concentrating on specific homes and families.

Quiet prayer walks complement more high-profile praise marches and prayer rallies. Worship and warfare blend with intercession that Christ will be welcomed as Lord by many throughout the entire city.

Prayerwalks give us a simple way to continually fill our streets with prayer. Many are praying city-size prayers. Thus we keep near our neighbors in order to touch our cities with the Good News. We tell them in our words and in our service.

Quiet triumphs often follow as God changes the city day by day and house by house.

HOW TO GET STARTED
"PRAYER WALKING"

JOIN WITH OTHER BELIEVERS. Join your faith with others to help prayer flow in an engaging conversational style. Large groups sometimes fail to give everyone a chance to participate. I encourage you to get together with two to four other people. If you have a larger group, divide into smaller groups. You will cover more area.

SET ASIDE TIME. Allow one or two hours, although much can be done in less time.

FOCUS ON GOD. Make God's promises rather than Satan's schemes the highlight of your prayers. Your discernment of evil powers may at times exceed God's specific guidance to engage them in direct combat.

RE-GATHER AND REPORT. Share what you are experiencing. Expressing something of your insights and faith will encourage others--as well as yourself. Set plans for further prayer walking.

COORDINATE EFFORTS. Enlist people in your group to prayer-walk with you. You may knock on the doors of your neighbors. In a kind way, tell them you are praying for them. The next time you walk you can stop by and ask how they are doing. When their prayers start being answered, they will be open to hear more! *(Portions of the above paragraphs are excerpted from Prayer Walking by Steve Hawthorne and Graham Kendrick—Creation House, 1993).*

Prayer walking and fasting go hand in hand. When Elijah fasted for 40 days, he walked from the desert to Mt. Horab. That was a prayer-walk. During our 21 days of fasting, I encourage you to walk your neighborhood, praying for people who live in your neighborhood. Use a theme passage of scripture. Use I Timothy 2:1-10. Verse eight speaks of the territorial dimension to prayer. The following prayer points emerge from this passage.

CONCERNING CHRIST: Proclaim Jesus afresh to be the Savior of all people. Name Him Lord of the neighborhood and of the lives you see.

CONCERNING PEACE: Cry out for the godliness and holiness of God's people to increase. Pray for new churches to be established.

CONCERNING THE GOSPEL: Celebrate the faithful revelation of Christ to all people (I Timothy 2:8). Pray for your friends and neighbors to come to know Christ. Name specific people. Name the people who live in homes. Their names may be on their mailboxes. Pray for God's message of hope to be displayed in the problems, tragedy, poverty, and dismay.

CONCERNING THE BLESSING OF GOD: Give thanks for the goodness God constantly bestows on the homes. Ask God to bring forth an enduring spiritual awakening.

CONCERNING THE CHURCH: Pray for relationships, that there be no wrath among God's people. Pray for God's people to be disciplined followers of Christ. Pray for worship to be expressed in faithful service and to be reflected in praise in the sanctuary.

OLD TESTAMENT: *Jonah 3:5-9*

CHAPTER 18

DAY 18

FASTING TO PROCLAIM LIBERTY AND TO HAVE FREEDOM FROM LEGALISM

An American Tradition. God heals YOU!
Luke 6 – 10

> *"Ye have lived in pleasure on the earth, and been wanton; ye have nourished your hearts, as in a day of slaughter."*
> *--James 5:5*

> *"Heal me, O LORD, and I shall be healed; save me, and I shall be saved: for thou art my praise."*
> *--Jeremiah 17:14*

Is fasting acceptable to contemporary Christian thinking? O. Hallesby certainly thought so and stated such in his book, **PRAYER**:

"Jesus did not abolish fasting, he lifted it from the legalism of the Old Covenant into the freedom of the New. Fasting is an outward act which should be carried out only when there is an inner need of it (Matthew 9:14-15). Furthermore, Jesus warns against fasting as a means of displaying piety, so as to be seen of men (Matthew 6:16-18).

"But should we fast?

"This is no doubt a live question in the minds of many Christians in our day. Many look upon fasting as a part of the outward ceremonialism which belonged only to the Old Covenant...That free, evangelical Christians should fast is entirely strange and foreign to their way of thinking.

"It is no doubt high time that we feeble, weak-willed and pleasure-loving Christians begin to see what the scriptures say concerning this element in our sanctification and in our prayer life.

"Fasting is not confined to abstinence from eating and drinking. Fasting really means voluntary abstinence for a time from various necessities of life such as food, drink, sleep, rest, association with people and so forth."

The purpose of such abstinence for a longer or shorter period of time is to loosen to some degree the ties which bind us to the world of material things and our surroundings as a whole, in order that we concentrate all our spiritual powers upon the unseen and eternal things.

To strive in prayer means in the final analysis to take up the battle against all the inner and outward hindrances which would disassociate us from the spirit of prayer.

There are many miracles that I have witnessed as people have fasted. These same miracles can happen in your life, too.

Jim Silvers worked outside as an automobile mechanic. During the worst winter in Kentucky's history, where the temperature did not get out of the teens for over one month, Jim fasted for 40 days. At the time, he wore glasses that were as thick as the bottoms of the old Coke bottles. At the end of the 40 days, God totally delivered him. God healed Jim's eyes to where he could see 20/20 without any glasses. At the same time, the Holy Spirit gave Jim a gift of writing music. Over 40 of his songs have been recorded by singing groups.

OLD TESTAMENT:

"And to speak unto the priests which were in the house of the LORD of hosts, and to the prophets, saying, Should I weep in the fifth month, separating myself, as I have done these so many years?
"Then came the word of the LORD of hosts unto me, saying, Speak unto all the people of the land, and to the priests, saying, When ye fasted and mourned in the fifth and seventh month, even those seventy years, did ye at all fast unto me, even to me?"
--Zechariah 7:3-5

CHAPTER 19

DAY 19

FASTING POSITIONS ONE FOR REPENTANCE

MERCY. Walk in God's mercy!
John 16 – 18

"Seeing therefore it remaineth that some must enter therein, and they to whom it was first preached entered not in because of unbelief:"
--Hebrews 4:6

At first, Jonah rebelled. But after three days in the belly of a fish, he repented and preached on the streets of Nineveh.

Our country has greatly sinned through homosexuality, abortion, exclusion of prayer and Bible reading from schools, humanism and numerous other national sins. We are becoming a Godless nation. Our only hope is through humbling ourselves to God through fasting and prayer. Nineveh's revival was short lived, because they ceased to seek God.

One hundred years later, Nahum the prophet declared destruction to the city of Nineveh. This was the mightiest city in the world with walls 100 feet high and wide enough to accommodate three chariots riding abreast. Dotted around the walls were huge towers that stretched another 100 feet above the huge walls. In addition, there was a mote around the city 150 feet wide and 60 feet deep. Nineveh appeared impregnable and could withstand a twenty-year siege.

Nahum predicted that Nineveh would end *"with an overflowing flood."* This is exactly what happened. The Tigris River overflowed its banks and the flood destroyed part of Nineveh's walls. The Babylonians invaded through the broken down walls and plundered and burned the city. Nahum also prophesied that the city would *"be hidden."* After its destruction in 612 B.C., the site was not discovered until 1842 A.D.

As you follow Jesus in fasting, you will realize God has a perfect plan for your life. Sometimes this is only revealed as you fast. Many wrong decisions in marriage or business could have been avoided if only God's perfect will would have been implemented.

There was a man who had gotten away from God. He was so discouraged that he had back-slidden. He talked to me, *"I just don't think that I can ever live for God."* I said, *"You can live for God and you can be an overcomer. We are getting ready to go on a 21-day fast; and I want you to fast with us."* He agreed. He fasted the whole 21 days. At the end of that time, God really established him, spiritually. God did something for him. It was like making steel for the back-bone to live for God.

Right after that, he met a girl. They fell in love. I performed their wedding. God blessed this couple. He started a new business. God gave them a home. God has multiplied His blessings to him. Now, he is one of the most faithful workers in the church that I have.

OLD TESTAMENT:

> *"Thus saith the LORD of hosts; The fast of the fourth month, and the fast of the fifth, and the fast of the seventh, and the fast of the tenth, shall be to the house of Judah joy and gladness, and cheerful feasts; therefore love the truth and peace."*
>
> *--Zechariah 8:19*

CHAPTER 20

DAY 20

FASTING AS A WAY OF LIFE

OVERCOMING TEMPTATION

We must overcome temptation and become bold for the Lord.

John 19 – 21

"The wicked flee when no man pursueth: but the righteous are bold as a lion."
--Proverbs 28:1

When Jesus fasted for 40 days, He was tempted by the devil. Often, when we fast, we think that we are so much closer to God that the devil will leave us alone. This is not true. I've been tempted more when I fast.

In fact, our spirits become more sensitive to the spirit world. Because of this, we can pick up and detect the demonic in a stronger manner. Often, we are less tolerant of the demonic. Sometimes we are more intolerant of our families who are involved in non-righteous activities than when we are not fasting.

Years ago, I was on a three-day fast without food or

water. A lady and her husband came to see me on the third day. They had been recommended by their pastor. I prayed for her. When I did, this demon manifested by picking her up and throwing her across my office. She landed on the floor. I got down beside her. Her husband was on one side; and I was on the other. We began to pray. These demons began to speak out of her. We prayed for her for over two hours until I could hardly talk.

That night, when I went home, I went to bed. In the middle of the night, my room began to shake. I thought we were experiencing a terrible storm. My wife woke up. I looked outside; and there was no storm at all. It was a spiritual storm in my room. This demon spoke to me. The demon said, "You stay out of the deliverance ministry or I will kill you!" Then every sin or wrong thing that I had done in my life seemed to flash before me. If I hadn't understood the righteousness of God, and the victory we have over the devil, I would not have been able to combat Satan.

The thought came to my mind that He could have called ten thousand angels. So I said that I wanted ten thousand angels in this room right now! When I did, my room became electrified with the presence of angels. It was as if I took a nylon shirt, and you could see the static electricity when I would shake it. That is how my room looked.

I began to prophesy of the coming of Christ, and that the Antichrist was alive in the world today. God gave us a great victory.

God will give you a great victory also, in every temptation you may face.

CHAPTER 21

DAY 21

BELIEVE GOD FOR A
100-FOLD BLESSING!

Believe God for great financial blessings. Jesus said we could be blessed 30, 60, and 100 fold.

"And every one that hath forsaken houses, or brethren, or sisters, or father, or mother, or wife, or children, or lands, for my name's sake, shall receive an hundredfold, and shall inherit everlasting life."
--Matthew 19:29

"And Jesus answered and said, Verily I say unto you, There is no man that hath left house, or brethren, or sisters, or father, or mother, or wife, or children, or lands, for my sake, and the gospel's, But he shall receive an hundredfold now in this time, houses, and brethren, and sisters, and mothers, and children, and lands, with persecutions; and in the world to come eternal life. But many that are first shall be last; and the last first."
--Mark 10:29-31

"Then Peter said, Lo, we have left all, and followed thee. And he said unto them, Verily I say unto

you, There is no man that hath left house, or parents, or brethren, or wife, or children, for the kingdom of God's sake, Who shall not receive manifold more in this present time, and in the world to come life everlasting."

--Luke 18:28-30

Which one do you choose? I choose 100-fold. Let me tell you what this means. What is the real meaning of a hundredfold blessing? It means 100 times. But does it mean double? It is easy to understand what thirty-fold and sixty-fold mean. Thirty-fold means thirty times, and sixty-fold simply means sixty times. But a hundredfold is much different.

Hundredfold is significant, for one hundred is a unique number. It is the only number that can represent every other number. It means the best possible. If you are a student and you take a test with 25 questions and get them all right you get 100. You can't do better than that. If there are 50 questions and you get them all correct you still get 100 percent.

If you are in the farming business and plant apple trees, how do you get a hundredfold blessing?

The average apple contains five seeds. If a hundredfold blessing was 100 times, you would only get twenty apples. However, we know apple trees live many years and can produce 5,000 or more apples. Accordingly, a hundredfold blessing could easily equal 25,000 times (five seeds per apple times 5,000 apples = 25,000 apple seeds). A hundred fold blessing means God will bless you the very best in your position.

If you work at McDonalds, you can rise to the top at

that position. If the top is a foreman, then that is where God can bless you. Sometimes people lose their jobs to find God is really promoting them. They could not rise any higher at their present position.

In Matthew 6 Jesus talks about giving (verse 3), praying (verses 6 and 7), and fasting (verses 16 and 17). In Matthew 6:18, Jesus said, *"And your Father who sees in secret will reward you openly."*

There is an individual blessing for each of these commandments. They all stand alone. There is a blessing when one gives, even if they don't pray. There is a blessing if one prays, and doesn't give or fast. Each of these alone gives a 30-fold blessing.

When you do two of these – pray and give – God blesses you sixty-fold. However, when you do all three – give, pray, and fast – it releases a hundred-fold blessing!

At the end of your fast, plant a seed. This is a financial amount that God puts in your heart. Plant a seed that costs you something. There have been times God has given me a figure and it has taken me months to pay it. At the end God blessed me greater than I ever thought possible.

Believe God for a hundred-fold blessing!

EPILOGUE

BREAKING THE FAST

I'm sure you have been thinking of eating. Many times as I've come to the end of a long fast, I wasn't really hungry. But unless God has spoken to you to go on--end your fast.

You must be very, very careful in doing so. It is extremely dangerous to break your fast with a large meal. I suggest you do not eat anything a baby would not eat. Start with juices that are diluted. Straight juice has too much acid and will burn your mouth and stomach.

You can eat oatmeal, chicken broth and soups. I've eaten soft-boiled eggs at times. The rule is you take as much time to break your fast, especially in getting back to eat meat, based upon the length of the fast.

Years ago a man in our church broke the 21-day fast with a large Italian meal. The grease would not process through his sleeping gall bladder. He went to the hospital. They removed his gall bladder, which put a strain on the heart. A couple of days later he died of a heart attack.

People do not die from fasting. They die from eating. Do not destroy your great spiritual victory by not being wise when you break your fast.

You must realize that during this time of fasting, your bowels have been dormant. To regain your regularity, soft foods with fiber should be eaten. Often, people just coming off a fast hurt themselves by eating harder foods. Harder foods can injure one's digestive tract. Extreme caution should be used as you begin to eat.

As you have won a great, spiritual victory in your fasting, do not think that Satan will step back and let you keep the new ground you gained without a fight. He won't. In fact, every time I come off of a fast, I have faced an attack of the enemy.

The day after I completed a 21-day fast, my daughter called me crying. Our beautiful Golden Retriever had gotten into a fight with a pack of dogs. They had, seemingly, bit his eye out. When I got home, the dog was so cut up and bleeding, I didn't think that he would live. When I took him to the veterinarian, the first thing he said was, "Your dog has lost its' eye."

A few minutes later, he came out and said, "As I was feeling his face, I felt an eyeball underneath the skin." The dogs bit around his eye and pulled the skin out from it. He was not optimistic that his eye could be saved.

I mentioned this on the phone to a friend of mine who was having a miracle crusade in Canada. Later that night he called on his cell phone and left a message that I did not retrieve until the next day. He told me that evening during the service there were three people that had been healed of blindness. When he got back to his room, the Spirit of God was still on him. The Lord spoke to him that the Lord wanted to heal my dog's eye.

He proceeded to pray a ten-minute prayer that my dog's eye would be healed. As I listened to the prayer, it really touched me that somebody would pray for my dog. So I went to the dog hospital. As my dog was lying there in the cage, I held the phone to his ear and played the prayer. He didn't move a muscle. Finally, when the prayer ended, and he said "Amen," my dog started barking. We prayed for him; and his eye was spared.

The Lord spoke to me through this, that when Satan attacks, it always looks worse than it really is. I had thought my dog was going to have to be put to sleep. But he recovered and was totally fine.

Satan will attack you. But always remember, it always looks worse than it really is. God will bring you to victory. Don't lose what God has given to you through these 21 days of prayer and fasting. Don't lose the victories that God has given you!

As you focus on Him
through your time of fasting,
it is my earnest prayer that
God will speak to you
and literally transform
your entire life
and family!

NOTES:

NOTES:

For more information about prayer and fasting books and tapes with Pastor Bob Rodgers, contact him today at:

Bob Rodgers Ministries
P.O. Box 19229
Louisville, KY 40259

www.worldprayercenter.org

For information on how to join the World Prayer Force and your free copy of the WORLD PRAYER FORCE REPORT, contact Pastor Bob Rodgers at:

www.PrayerRadio.net

Fasting & Prayer Books

By Bob Rodgers

Bob Rodgers
World Prayer Force

P.O. Box 19229
Louisville, Kentucky 40259
(502) 964-3304 EXT. 133

Books:

101 Reasons to Fast	$ 8.00
21 Days of Fasting	$10.00
Patterns of Prayer	$ 6.00
How to Pray the Lord's Prayer	$10.00
Miracle Book	$12.00
How Col. Sanders Found His Wealth	$ 2.00
How to Get Out of Debt in 50 Days	$10.00
5 Reasons Why People Do Not Fast	$ 6.00

Name: _____

Address: _____

City: _____ State: _____ Zip: _____

Phone: _____ E-Mail: _____

Amount of Purchase   **Method of Payment**

Sub Total _____   Check ___ Cash ___

Tax _____   Credit Card: AmEx ___

Grand Total _____   Discover ___ MC ___ Visa ___

KY Residents Add 6% Tax

Card No. & Exp. Date _____

Card Holder's Name (Please Print) _____

Card Holder's Signature _____

PRODUCT ORDER FORM

To contact Pastor Bob Rodgers on the Internet:

www.worldprayercenter.org

www.PrayerRadio.net

If this book has been a blessing to you, please let me know.

Bob Rodgers Ministries
Box 19229
Louisville, KY 40259

www.worldprayercenter.org

www.PrayerRadio.net